A Gleam in the Eye

Books by Louis Daniel Brodsky

Poetry

Five Facets of Myself   (1967)* (1995)

The Easy Philosopher   (1967)* (1995)

"A Hard Coming of It" and Other Poems   (1967)* (1995)

The Foul Rag-and-Bone Shop   (1967)* (1969, exp.)* (1995, exp.)

Points in Time   (1971)* (1995) (1996)

Taking the Back Road Home   (1972)* (1997) (2000)

Trip to Tipton and Other Compulsions   (1973)* (1997)

"The Talking Machine" and Other Poems   (1974)* (1997)

Tiffany Shade   (1974)* (1997)

Trilogy: A Birth Cycle   (1974) (1998)

Cold Companionable Streams   (1975)* (1999)

Monday's Child   (1975) (1998)

Preparing for Incarnations   (1975)* (1976, exp.) (1999) (1999, exp.)

The Kingdom of Gewgaw   (1976) (2000)

Point of Americas II   (1976) (1998)

La Preciosa   (1977) (2001)

Stranded in the Land of Transients   (1978) (2000)

The Uncelebrated Ceremony of Pants-Factory Fatso   (1978) (2001)

Birds in Passage   (1980) (2001)

Résumé of a Scrapegoat   (1980) (2001)

Mississippi Vistas: Volume One of A Mississippi Trilogy   (1983) (1990)

You Can't Go Back, Exactly   (1988, two eds.) (1989) (2003, exp.)

The Thorough Earth   (1989)

Four and Twenty Blackbirds Soaring   (1989)

Falling from Heaven: Holocaust Poems of a Jew and a Gentile (with William Heyen)   (1991)

Forever, for Now: Poems for a Later Love   (1991)

Mistress Mississippi: Volume Three of A Mississippi Trilogy   (1992)

A Gleam in the Eye: Volume One of The Seasons of Youth   (1992) (2009)

Gestapo Crows: Holocaust Poems   (1992)

The Capital Café: Poems of Redneck, U.S.A.   (1993)

Disappearing in Mississippi Latitudes: Volume Two of A Mississippi Trilogy   (1994)

A Mississippi Trilogy: A Poetic Saga of the South   (1995)*

Paper-Whites for Lady Jane: Poems of a Midlife Love Affair   (1995)

The Complete Poems of Louis Daniel Brodsky: Volume One, 1963–1967
  (edited by Sheri L. Vandermolen)   (1996)

Three Early Books of Poems by Louis Daniel Brodsky, 1967–1969: The Easy Philosopher,
  "A Hard Coming of It" and Other Poems, and The Foul Rag-and-Bone Shop
  (edited by Sheri L. Vandermolen)   (1997)

The Eleventh Lost Tribe: Poems of the Holocaust   (1998)

Toward the Torah, Soaring: Poems of the Renascence of Faith   (1998)

Voice Within the Void: Poems of *Homo supinus*   (2000)

Rabbi Auschwitz: Poems Touching the Shoah   (2000)*

The Swastika Clock: Endlösung Poems   (2001)*

Shadow War: A Poetic Chronicle of September 11 and Beyond, Volume One   (2001) (2004)

The Complete Poems of Louis Daniel Brodsky: Volume Two, 1967–1976
  (edited by Sheri L. Vandermolen)   (2002)

Shadow War: A Poetic Chronicle of September 11 and Beyond, Volume Two   (2002) (2004)

Shadow War: A Poetic Chronicle of September 11 and Beyond, Volume Three   (2002) (2004)

Shadow War: A Poetic Chronicle of September 11 and Beyond, Volume Four   (2002) (2004)

Shadow War: A Poetic Chronicle of September 11 and Beyond, Volume Five   (2002) (2004)

Heavenward   (2003)*

Regime Change: Poems of America's Showdown with Iraq, Volume One   (2003)*

Regime Change: Poems of America's Showdown with Iraq, Volume Two   (2003)*

Regime Change: Poems of America's Showdown with Iraq, Volume Three   (2003)*

The Complete Poems of Louis Daniel Brodsky: Volume Three, 1976–1980
  (edited by Sheri L. Vandermolen)   (2004)

Peddler on the Road: Days in the Life of Willy Sypher   (2005)

Combing Florida's Shores: Poems of Two Lifetimes   (2006)

Showdown with a Cactus: Poems Chronicling the Prickly Struggle Between the Forces
  of Dubya-ness and Enlightenment, 2003–2006   (2006)

A Transcendental Almanac: Poems of Nature   (2006)

Once upon a Small-Town Time: Poems of America's Heartland   (2007)

Still Wandering in the Wilderness: Poems of the Jewish Diaspora   (2007)

The Location of the Unknown: Shoah Poems   (2008)*

The World Waiting to Be: Poems About the Creative Process   (2008)

The Complete Poems of Louis Daniel Brodsky: Volume Four, 1981–1985
  (edited by Sheri L. Vandermolen)   (2008)

Dine-Rite: Breakfast Poems   (2008)

Kampf: Poems of the Holocaust   (2009)*

Bibliography *(coedited with Robert Hamblin)*

Selections from the William Faulkner Collection of Louis Daniel Brodsky: A Descriptive
  Catalogue   (1979)

Faulkner: A Comprehensive Guide to the Brodsky Collection: Volume I, The Biobibliography   (1982)

Faulkner: A Comprehensive Guide to the Brodsky Collection: Volume II, The Letters   (1984)

Faulkner: A Comprehensive Guide to the Brodsky Collection: Volume III, *The De Gaulle Story*   (1984)

Faulkner: A Comprehensive Guide to the Brodsky Collection: Volume IV, *Battle Cry*   (1985)

Faulkner: A Comprehensive Guide to the Brodsky Collection: Volume V, Manuscripts and
  Documents   (1989)

Country Lawyer and Other Stories for the Screen by William Faulkner   (1987)

Bibliography *(coedited with Robert Hamblin) (continued)*

Stallion Road: A Screenplay by William Faulkner   (1989)

Biography

William Faulkner, Life Glimpses   (1990)

Fiction

Between Grief and Nothing *(novel)*   (1964)*

Between the Heron and the Wren *(novel)*   (1965)*

"Dink Phlager's Alligator" and Other Stories   (1966)*

The Drift of Things *(novel)*   (1966)*

Vineyard's Toys *(novel)*   (1967)*

The Bindle Stiffs *(novel)*   (1968)*

Yellow Bricks *(short fictions)*   (1999)

Catchin' the Drift o' the Draft *(short fictions)*   (1999)

This Here's a Merica *(short fictions)*   (1999)

Leaky Tubs *(short fictions)*   (2001)

Rated Xmas *(short fictions)*   (2003)

Nuts to You! *(short fictions)*   (2004)

Pigskinizations *(short fictions)*   (2005)

Memoir

The Adventures of the Night Riders, Better Known as the Terrible Trio
   (with Richard Milsten)   (1961)*

* *Unpublished*

A Gleam in the Eye

Volume One of *The Seasons of Youth*

poems by
Louis Daniel Brodsky

An imprint of Time Being Press
St. Louis, Missouri

Time Being Books®
10411 Clayton Road
St. Louis, Missouri 63131

Time Being Books® is an imprint of Time Being Press®, St. Louis, Missouri.

Time Being Press® is a 501(c)(3) not-for-profit corporation.

Time Being Books® volumes are printed on acid-free paper.

ISBN 978-1-56809-127-3 (paperback)

Library of Congress Cataloging-in-Publication Data:

Brodsky, Louis Daniel.
    A gleam in the eye : poems / by Louis Daniel Brodsky. — 2nd ed.
        p. cm. — (The seasons of youth ; v. 1)
    ISBN: 978-1-56809-127-3 (pbk. : alk. paper)
    1. First pregnancy—Poetry. 2. Parenthood—Poetry. 3.
Infants—Poetry. 4. Parent and infant—Poetry. I. Title.
    PS3552.R623G54 2009
    811'.54—dc22
                                                    2009023283

Cover design by Jeff Hirsch
Front cover artwork by Jan Hofmann Brodsky. Courtesy of the artist.
Book design and typesetting by Trilogy M. Mattson

Manufactured in the United States of America

Second Edition, first printing (2009)

Acknowledgments

I am very grateful to Sheri Vandermolen and to Jerry Call, Editor in Chief and Managing Editor, respectively, of Time Being Books, for their perceptive improvements to these poems as they appeared in the 1992 edition of this book, which they worked on as well. My thanks to them, for helping me bring to fruition the original vision I had for this book.

To my daughter, Trilogy Maya Mattson, a special thank you, for her close reading, her suggestions, and, above all, for having been and for being, yet, the inspiration for these poems.

Certain pieces in this book have appeared, in different versions, in the following magazines: *Art Times* ("Father's Den"); *Kansas Quarterly* ("Suggestions"); *Main Street Rag* ("Conception," as "Conception: A Recollection"); *Midwest Poetry Review* ("Paean to Jan and Trilogy"); *Phase and Cycle* ("Crocheting Solomon's Seal"); *Route One* ("Conception," as "Conception: A Recollection"); *South Carolina Review* ("The Mutoscope" and "Our Song"); and *Whetstone* ("Eye in the Sky").

For Jan Hofmann Brodsky,

who shared, with me,
the sacred privilege of bestowing life
on Trilogy and Troika,
the most precious, blessed legacies of our love

Our birth is but a sleep and a forgetting:
The Soul that rises with us, our life's Star,
Hath had elsewhere its setting,
And cometh from afar:
Not in entire forgetfulness,
And not in utter nakedness,
But trailing clouds of glory do we come
From God, who is our home:
Heaven lies about us in our infancy!

— William Wordsworth, "Ode: Intimations of
Immortality from Recollections of Early Childhood"

Contents

Coming to Terms

Birth

A New Home

Eyeing the World

Exercising Rites

Growing Familiar

A Gleam in the Eye

Coming to Terms

Conception

While we visit Illinois relatives
So distant from our home in Farmington,
The beginning of life surfaces,
In our primal psyches,
As primitivistically
As superstition in a savage
Worshiping the moon's phases.
We prepare to do rituals
To the gods of fertility and birth.

Blissfully, we sit,
Listening to each other's heartbeats
Echoing babies
Breathing within babies
Echoing inside babies
Seeking peaceful regions
In amniotic caves,
Where they can safely be born
Into life's wakeful sleep and forgetting.

Now, like twilight leaving the sky,
For a prior universe,
We fly to day's edge,
To monitor the earth's pulse.
Soon, we'll dive into its bloodstream,
Beneath wine-scented sleep,
And hope to discover, in our lovemaking,
Creation's secret:
Conception immaculately sweet.

The Moment

As seething daylight expands toward night,
On invisible mind-vines,
Everything takes on the tumid saturation
Of overripe fruit.
Rain contained in the humid air
Fills the sky,
With seeds sweeping by, overhead,
Like snow geese in flight,
Penetrating bright-white ova.

All these exalted shapes,
Animate and numinous,
Poise just long enough to imbue the horizon,
With the mysterious symmetry of their being.
Something has set them free,
As if the rain might be godly sperm
Spontaneously impregnating her.
At once, she senses, in her lush fecundity,
The inception of a child.

Continuities: A Dream

One child,
Born of two mild children of God,
Tiptoes over stones made of years,
Painstakingly placed,
At strategic spots in the stream,
To make crossing easier
And keep the journeyer from getting wet.

Not questioning his motives,
He's refused to settle into patterns
Leading to tragedy,
Never stepped, precariously, into the water,
In his escapes from wild creatures
That threaten his blessed,
Ineffable contrariness.

Only the hope of finding a helpmate
Sustains his lonely flight
Through a forest deeper than life,
Wider than the highest banks
That rise along the stream he contemplates.
Suddenly, her reflection, on the surface,
Sees him seeking, reaching,

And brings him to his knees.
She receives his kiss, in silence.
Two mild children of God
Dissolve into their own reflection,
Meet their ageless parents,
Where the stream originates, beneath earth.
Circles fan out like rosebuds opening,

Then close upon their union.
The family assembles, to consecrate a birth.
A naked child emerges,
Then tiptoes away, over stones made of years,
Submerged below her.
Walking on water, unafraid, unscathed,
She crosses the stream, alone.

Adoration

Reborn,
Seeing before the beginning,
Breathing love songs
Composed along the way,
We fly back, together,
Through vast expanses,
To glory-washed predestiny.

We sing a child into being —
Conceiving three
From one unification of two —
Borrowed from many souls
Resurrected from prior lives
Controlled by order
Older than time.

Roaming through jasmine fields
Laced with gardenias,
We sleep in one dream,
Dreaming a trinity,
Two fantasies
Mingled with borzois, ginkgoes,
Wishing-trees, and iridescent fish.

Flying easterly, peacefully,
We inhale celestial vapors,
As we slip, naked, through space,
Wending our way home —
From nonexistent to triumvirate,
In one inspiration,
Two humans approximating God.

Crocheting Solomon's Seal

For her, the needles crochet melody
And intertwine hopes,
In a perpetual easing of tensions.
Caught up in her fingers' movements,
My eyes are mesmerized
By spiraling light unwinding from skeins
Of brightly dyed yarns;
My wife's concentrate on the design.

Naked on our bed, together,
Sighing contentedly,
Free from prying eyes, for a while,
We rejoice in the dazzlement of creation,
As though silence were the embryo
Growing inside her womb,
The placenta a bunting,
A holy robe, a godly seal of Solomon.

Solomon's seal: an emblem consisting of two interlaced triangles form-
ing a six-pointed star, symbolic of the union of two souls

Putting in the Garden

The snorting engine,
Mounted to the welded tubular frame
Of my red, chain-driven tiller,
Is the head of a horse
That doesn't even sweat,
As the hooves of my modern plow
Unknot earth and churn it up.

The reins of this machine
Connect my pounding blood with nature,
Which waits patiently for me,
As I labor to persuade
One of man's mechanical contrivances
To help me create, from the land,
A cornucopia of fruits and vegetables.

From printed packets,
I take seed after seed after seed,
Drop each into furrows I've hoed,
Row by row,
And cover it with fertile dirt,
My fingers pirouetting like ballerinas
Across a dusty stage.

Finishing my task diminishes me.
My overalls are stained at the knees.
My limbs shake from fatigue.
Romantic notions of growth and harvest fade,
Like labels tacked to stakes.
Sweat dries on my gold-rimmed glasses.
I grope for the patch's unfenced edge.

As I leave our garden,
An image of Demeter, in my wife's likeness,
Or my wife, in her ageless simplicity,
Ripening, fast, toward the last hours
Of her nine-month cycle,
Slowly approaches,
To hallow the completion of my planting.

Last Days Before the First Baby

How outlandish the dream that precedes birth,
Heralding its newborn, among the quick.
In the beginning,
An early spring continues perpetually.
A heart beats in sweet sympathy
With another blood it washes clean,
Until both expectant lady
And her astonished husband
Are left floating, breathlessly,
Within a gossamer sweep of gravity,
As her swelling belly
Achieves jubilant tumescence.

All these wordless urges surge toward release,
From the divine scripture
Stored, like a Torah,
In the fleshly ark of his wife's ripe temple.
The dream becomes fetus,
The child natural law
Reality keeps balanced with death.
Soon, their conception of life,
Moving further downstream,
Will break through the opening,
Into a glorious new ocean
Filled with a mother's radiant tears.

Birth

The Pearl

Slowly, the grit developed,
Within the host's quiet enclosure,
Beneath the ultimate silence its sea emitted.
No foreign bodies penetrated the shell,
As the grain began spinning,
About its silvery self,
A seamless web
Protecting its delicate heart and brain.

Now, the vessel is straining to break open,
Release its precious possession,
That others might see themselves
Reflected in the pearl's perfection.

Vestiges

The alchemy of bodily change
Arranges a passageway
Out of the grotto,
For safe escape from the ocean
In which the floating being has survived,
Without breathing through nose or mouth,
For fully three seasons.

Very soon,
It will leave the maternal heat,
Have earthly air
Introduced into its collapsed lungs,
And open its eyes, to first light,
After a midnight odyssey
That's lasted clockless eons.

Such rituals as these,
Visionary gleams of glorious dreams
Existing in distant worlds,
Are the only vestiges
We're privileged to see
Before all heavenly trappings fall away
And the routine feeding begins.

Crew Practice

I move from obstetrician's office,
    in midtown St. Louis,
To crew shell,
    beyond New Haven's ghettos,
At Derby, on the Housatonic,
    floating upstream, twelve years,
On memory's murky surface,
    back to all those daily practices
For Saturday races,
    recalling discipline, courage,
Fatigue, and nervous nights
    leading to this day . . .
The momentum of steady blades
    recovering across choppy waves;
Breaking the finish line first;
    holding the trophy shirt
Over my shoulders — a baby,
    with whom I'll do my training
When the last regatta is forgotten.

Inducement

Now that the fetus has finally reached full term,
We've been given the dubious choice
Of selecting induced or natural labor.
If the former is followed through,
To its elemental conclusion,
God's ordained stride of childbirth
Will be significantly altered,
And we'll assume sole responsibility
For severing heavenly ties with predestiny.

Cutting the umbilical cord prematurely
Might break weak links in the chain of being,
Disturb life's rhythms and balance.
Besieged by this awesome option to preempt nature
And mandated, by free will,
To arrive at a viable plan for our designs,
We come to the decision, diffidently,
To initiate parturition
And start the breath of our waiting child.

Father's Den

Beyond the massive walnut doors,
They've taken my wife,
Taken my wife,
Beyond the massive walnut doors.
Two slabs of a tree and a shiny corridor
Separate the space,
Keep us from seeing each other,
Form a barrier
Between trepidation and joyous expectation.

As I wait to join my wife, in the labor room,
Amnesia and paranoia set in,
And I feel myself beginning to spin,
Forget where I am,
Where we are, together,
Separately,
Both waiting for the doors to swing open
And readmit us
Into the private world we've shared.

Debut

Nurses and attendants in blue gowns,
Doctors in green scrubs,
And I, standing in the background,
Peer, above surgical masks,
At my blond wife between sheets,
Periodically read line graphs
Projecting, like soliloquies,
From the lips of Fetal Monitor 101B —
Two nervous tongues
Squeaking out heartbeats and contractions,
As if registering tremors from an earthquake,
Not intervals and intensities
Of a mother and her baby
Begging for release.

From a clear bag,
Pit continually drips, drips,
Through an IV in her pulsing wrist.
Too soon,
The contractions assume a new magnitude,
Require prepared breathing,
As effacement evolves, from hurried dilation,
Into hasty transition —
Three centimeters to eight, in two hours.
Then she's moved into the delivery room,
Transferred, from rolling bed,
To stationary operating table,
With stainless-steel tools on nearby trays,
The whole tableau in a glowing halo.

Suddenly, she seems ready
To participate in a sacred act of marriage
Between herself and God.
These vows involve her
In a surging push toward a liberation
No machine can record
Nor doctor prolong,
As the natal ceremony concludes.
First, the head emerges;
The body advances one bloody limb at a time;
Then life cord, placenta,
A whimper — debut . . .
The hour, the place, the day,
Forever commemorated.

First Feedings

The new baby
Has moved from her divine environs
And, with His permission,
Taken up residence in our purlieus.
With her strong sucking needs,
Feeding becomes a ceaseless seeking
Of the stores of warm colostrum.
Setting up an effective expression of sustenance,
With her loving mother,
Is the chief reason for her pilgrimages
From nursery to nurturing life source.
No longer is existence umbilical,
Though dependence persists,
With this imminent difference:
Soon, the child, like her mother already,
Will be beholden, for nourishment,
Solely to God.

Heavenly Bodies

From minutiae, our two specks grew —
Moon chasing sun,
Sun moon,
One dependent upon the other,
Both nearly invisible,
Though emitting dim emanations
From the fiery core of the Source we orbit.

Our union fostered a new hope
Of sustaining,
In man's earthly garden,
The tenderly shaped bloom
Of human kindness.
Soon, a godly image emerged
As womb fruit,
Ripened,
And blossomed into a third speck,
Resembling flesh of our respective flesh.

This day,
We've come to acclaim
Trilogy Maya.
She's the newest moon
In a galaxy defined by love
Edging ever outward.
Her birth connects us with Genesis.

Trilogy

A tiny, resplendent enterprise,
Like a low moon
Steadily rising over the horizon,
Enlarged, gradually, in her womb,
Which grew in proportion
To the glowing life floating within.

Her abdomen's thin skin
Stretched like twilight,
Became as translucent as blue sky
Flowing through the eyes of God.
Tremors from the core
Periodically distorted the basic shape.

Atoms continually rearranged themselves,
As the being moved, actively,
Toward peaceful release,
From a world shrinking, by subtle degrees,
Even as it expanded
Toward blessed coalescence.

Finally, confinement unloosed its hold,
And silence divided,
Like ocean waves breaking close.
A child rode in, at high tide,
And exploded against our beach,
Crying as if relieved

To have arrived from a journey
Taking many millenniums.
Amazed, my wife and I gazed
Not in disbelief
But colossal wonderment,
At a conception fleshed into wet reality.

Today, our two separate identities,
Fused by love,
Have been transformed,
Made whole,
In a covenant of pure earthly worship —
Three equal parts, indivisible.

Going to the Land of Canaan

Itchy stitches; mother's milk;
Lingering tinges of jaundice;
The nurse's final reminders
On feeding, bathing, holding,
Supporting the head;
Bouquets and extravagant arrangements
In various stages of decay.
Our preparations to leave
Began by midweek,
And now, as Sabbath arrives,
We anticipate transplanting our new flower
To a garden far away.

The city may be a safe place for being born,
But, ah, for breathing,
The country is, ineluctably,
Sweeter and cleaner.
And so we head home, at first light,
No longer alone, as we arrived,
Beguiled, now, by the fascinating wiles
Of a Trilogy we've conceived,
A mystically born force
Reaching deeply to touch us with meaning
And redeem our longing souls
From incompleteness.

A New Home

Paean to Jan and Trilogy

Eyes closed,
Nose pressed against the breast
Of her nursing mother,

Our baby rests
In eternal caress, a nested bird
Expecting sustenance

From its protectress.
Such liquescent godliness
Can hardly be expressed

By her cooing and peeps.
The miracle leaps from the mirror,
Reflecting preciousness,

Onto her body,
Suckling from the earth's core.
The poetry of her birth

Confirms God.
The immediacy of her tiny feet
And uneven breathing

Reminds me
How we three are netted
In overlapping metaphors

Of seizing time
And squeezing dry the ripest fruit,
To taste the primal milk —

From my rib, my wife;
From her lush garden,
Our daughter, Trilogy.

Flower-Laced Trellis and Lilacs

The day is a friendly face greeting us,
Through flower-laced trellis, beyond lilacs,
A neighborly smile
From a family we know
Only for an occasional pleasantry,
A wave-of-the-hand day
Floating through welcoming purlieus,
Like a dream escaping a dream
Coinciding with our arrival
To celebrate baby Trilogy's advent,
In this end-of-May Xanadu.

From now on,
Our time is hers.
We'll be her progressing moments,
The provisional hours
Toward which her hands will point,
As she follows each new sunrise, to sunset,
Over destiny's clock dial,
Growing in our gleaming eyes,
While she gazes, through flower-laced trellis,
Beyond lilacs, at the friendly face
Waiting to take her away someday.

Thanking Dr. Long

Dear Dr. Long,

For the last four weeks,
During the craziest hours of the night,
Jan and I
Have thought and thought
About what we could present to you,
For making us three.

We decided that what you might like
Is a new flight jacket,
This navy blazer with contrast stitching,
So you can fly into Farmington or St. Louis
Without having to change
To attend any occasion.

If it needs slight adjustment,
Just fill out a flight plan,
Check moisture in the wing tanks,
Reset your altimeter, crank the prop,
And take off for the country.
You name the day — any day at all.

We both hope
You'll soar like a sunray,
In your new aviator's garb,
As high as our spirits have flown
Since the thirteenth of May,
When you guided Trilogy in, on instruments.

> With love,
>
> The new parents

First Father's Day

Composing a greeting card
To be mailed special delivery,
I discover something illuminating,
An essence shared
With one of my parents,
As I write, "Dear Dad,
Now that *I* have a child,
I can empathize with you;
I know what fatherhood means.

"On this glorious day,
As you and I look toward creation,
We cast back, to that day
When the first member of our family
Lay cradled beneath the tree
Shading our history.
My new baby has made me appreciate
That we're all begotten
Of the same godly seed."

Our Song

How can music
Be so churchly serene
That it makes me kneel
On cold stone floors and weep?
The song I hear
Is my wife and child
Lying together, both asleep.
Each breath they share
Releases a sweet note
Scored by me,
Devotedly,
As I tiptoe from our bedroom,
To keep from waking them.
All afternoon,
My eyes hymn our melody.

Ex Utero

Our tiny baby rests silently,
In a womb of human activity.
No longer does fluid
Insulate her from pollutants
We reluctantly breathe,
Nor do we celebrate her, daily,
With bouquets of fragile flowers
And crocheted lace.

She is Trilogy Maya,
A rain forest of orchids
Blooming profusely in her face.
Her smooth flesh
Is a velvet nativity robe
Almost too delicate to touch,
Like the mist of a soft summer rain.
Her soul is His sacred memento.

Now, as I gaze upon her helplessness,
Tears well up behind my eyes.
I know her new home
Is but a sleep and a forgetting,
During which we bear complete responsibility
For keeping God's covenant.
Ours, we realize, is a sacred privilege
We mustn't, for heaven's sake, forsake.

The Kingdom of Innocence

The widest eyes in the kingdom
Reside in her face,
Reveal a princess owing allegiance
To the ruler who feeds her,
My devoted wife,
Her regal queen/mother.
The stores, fortified with love,
Will endure another reign;
Her realm is secure.

Now, her eyes close on dreams
She resurrects
From memories bequeathed from above.
A fortress rises.
When she opens her lids again —
Those twin portcullises —
Jan and I will enter
And spend the rest of our lives with her,
Safe inside.

Waiting for the Final Release

Proud new parents,
We sit in Dr. Long's waiting room,
Our baby lying quietly
On my wife's swaying knees.
Soon, Jan will be checked internally,
On this, her final postpartum visit,
Then joyously released.

Both of us vividly remember,
Through glorious reverie,
Another occasion we waited here,
Anxious as actors taking the stage,
Just us then,
United against the unknown,
Come to behold an impending delivery.

Now, ten weeks have elapsed,
And a desperate sense of helplessness
Overwhelms our tense minds,
Bends our selfish misconceptions,
Exaggerates our fears
Of the fragility of Trilogy's spirit,
Which arrived like a heavenly knell.

Frightened, we reassure ourselves
Only a misanthrope could repudiate this gift,
Forget that He who exhales death
Has also breathed, equally inscrutably,
Into the shape of our sleeping baby,
A divine design that inspires
By reminding us our lives are constantly cycling.

Eyeing the World

Beginning to See

Converging in front of her eyes,
Blurs burn through haze,
Then come into scintillating focus.
She grows a blink at a time.
Objects change into persons
Rearranging noises she'll interpret
As voices and other sounds.

Rotating joints
Become mesmeric points
On which her mind pivots
And draws inward
All the colossal weight of shapes,
Rarefied on the cathedraled air,
She'll one day use to move the earth.

Those perceiving the baby
As a maker of grave decisions
Know that, to her,
Choice is the flat, red side
Of a round, white toy
Turned obliquely, like a metaphor,
To reveal an innovative insight.

Now, her blue eyes,
Which, at birth,
Looked through murky pupils,
Without distinguishing us,
Follow the circle of friendship we describe,
That concave silhouette of years
She'll fill with her love for us.

Her First Toy

The fleshy-legged baby
Lies blithely, on her back,
Her head, moving side to side,
Imitating the arc
A plastic rattle makes, above her crib.
White, yellow, and blue magic granules
Flow through the toy's neck,
Like ideas spraying the brain
Before taking shape.
Her three-month-old mind
Is mesmerized by the raucous sounds
And the wild-flying colors
Leaving one shimmering globe,
Reappearing in the other.

Seeing her own features
Mirrored in the sphere
At each end of time's toy,
Does she recognize memories of preexistence,
Or is her preciously reflected image
Just another brilliant bead
Arriving, fleetingly,
With each slow turn,
At a new place in an open space
In the rattle her dad playfully waves
In her dazzle-dizzied gaze?

Eye in the Sky

Sitting in her car seat,
She slowly opens her eyes.
Her groping pupils
Focus on crimson dawn
Viewed through tinted windows,
As she, our waking child,
Accompanies us, this twilight,
On our third trip together,
Far from the source of her birth.

She must trust us,
Just as we place blind faith
In directions we've been given,
Believing we'll arrive on time,
Eager to introduce Trilogy
To members of her extended family.
This drive into the sun's widening horizon
Doubtless reminds our child
Of her original journey and us of ours.

First Insights

Our child enraptures me, with her smiles.
Such smooth, unassuming contortions,
On a face as yet untrained
In deviltry,
Contain no seeds of pain or disillusionment.

Her wide grin is a sign of contentedness,
On recognizing herself and me
In my glinting, eager eyes.
We're perfect friends,
Accepting each other unconditionally.

One moment are we,
In the sum of two lifetimes.
Timelessly, we rub cheek to cheek,
Like rose petals fluttered by a breeze.
We've become not just playmates or acquaintances

But, without vacant smiles anymore,
Father and daughter, blended in embrace,
Who, on this occasion,
Seem to perceive a feature of the other
Both have failed to see before.

Novitiates

The baby speaks to me, in pantomime,
Singing lyrics transcribed by her eyes
And writing love notes,
With fingertips that gently pat my mustache.
She coos wisdoms
She's brought, from a distance,
To enlighten my blind-to-life mind.

I breathe in her ear,
Wait for words I've never dreamed
To escape like echoes
Spiraling from a conch shell.
My lips kiss her belly delicately,
As though it were a gardenia
That might wilt at the slightest touch.

So innocent and mild
Is the religion the child hymns,
Crying to be fed from her mother's breast.
Helplessly, this small priestess
Calls me to her altar.
In devout pantomime,
I weep adorations to her, sublimely.

Preliminaries

The baby sleeps
In steep, gleaming clouds
Crowded in eastern flower beds.
She dreams destinies conceived by God,
Climbs a stairway made of stars
Braided with time-webs,
To hold it firmly
During the first few years
Of the Earth-journey bequeathed her.

She stirs, turns her head,
Sighs quietly.
Symbols, like sand granules,
Stream by her hemispheres,
Toward interpretations yet evolving.
She is Trilogy Maya,
Our newborn being,
Whose unformulated brain
Patiently awaits final instructions
For her first voyage
To the bright side of the mind's full moon.

On Looking into Trilogy's Eyes

Into her blue, blue eyes I stare,
Entranced by antic reflections
Of my hair and handlebar mustache.
My unusual face,
Elongated as an El Greco saint's,
Floats in those two liquescent pools,
Like silvery moon shadows
Or golden notes from a shofar
Perpetually shaping
These days of secular reckoning
Into the song of my daughter and me.

We're each a piece of a holy seed,
Growing within a communal womb.
In her, I see myself as a bloom
Blossoming from age to age,
Family to genus to beautiful species,
In regenerative imitation
Of the ultimate God-conceived creation,
To which human speech is the key
That opens the mind's silence
And conscience the lock
That keeps the instincts boxed.

She's my home away from the home I abandoned,
On uprooting myself at birth,
Moving my quarters
To the teeming universe
Humans use as their way station.
I'm both her gentle landlord and tenant,
Remaining steadfast,
Night and day,
At the wrought gates of her eyes,
To guard against centaurs and satyrs
Disguised as nursery-rhyme Boy Blues.

As my bittersweet eyes
Strain to recognize my face in hers,
I imagine the hour
When I'll be sitting alone,
*

Without her irises of the bluest blue
In which to gaze, to remind myself
That the inhabitant of this chubby face,
Already suggesting my features,
Is a scion of heaven's flowering tree
As well as the precious daughter
Of my ecstasy.

Exercising Rites

At Five Months

Her savoring of food has finally moved,
By definite impressions,
From tongue, to brain,
Like arterial blood through veins, to heart.
Once, only mother's milk sufficed,
Then cereal mixed with formula.
Now, she's taught herself to hate peas,
Tolerate carrots and beans,
And devour apricots, peaches, and pears
As if each were her sweet sucking-thumb.

Tiny hands, having mastered grasping,
Not wholly by design or accident,
Are beginning to touch exotic objects.
Her stubby fingers are antennae
Trying to differentiate hot/cold,
Rough/smooth, sharp/soft/hard,
Dry/wet
Like diapers sullied willy-nilly
Or clean crib sheets
Soiled overnight, in her sweaty sleep.

We've seen her stiff-necked head
Begin to follow quick movements
Instinctively,
Perhaps just from fear
Of intruders bearing gifts.
She chooses who will hold her,
Refuses dignitaries.
Only her father, with his special voice,
And the gentle lady who breast-feeds her
Can soothe Trilogy Maya into quietude.

The Human Race

With cheers from her parents,
She shows no signs of wearying,
On passing the halfway marker,
In the cross-country meet
She entered six months ago,
When the contest was first announced.

To train, she practiced calisthenics, on her back,
Vigorously drawing her hands
Toward her face, then away,
To keep herself limber
And moving smoothly over rough terrain,
In the initial stages of the race.

She ended with sets of knee bends.
(After many attempts
To reach and grasp her kicking feet and toes,
She succeeded in holding the position,
While perception
Connected the act to memory.)

Now, she's at the head of the pack,
Its invisible multitudes lagging,
As the path she runs weaves a circuitous course,
Leading to a finish line
Toward which she intuitively heads,
To claim her victory over nonexistence.

Suggestions

Our growing cub
Is exploring the earth,
Touching, testing, groping,
Gumming whatever her ravenous hands
Can grasp
And draw into her mouth:
Pages of a convenient magazine,
Clean laundry,
Her mother's accessible breasts,
Heated to expectation,
And her own tasty thumb —
Every anything within reach.

As benefactors of an intellect
Evolved from divine silence,
A being in training,
We still wonder what gospel
Predicted this creativity,
Which disciple
Prophesied the coming of such purity.
Now, we know why her arrival
Was so vigilantly awaited.
Even today, we can only imagine
The paradise she left,
By the way she yet smiles in her sleep.

One-Woman Show

An old, faded quilt
Brought up from the basement
And thrown over the living-room rug
Is a playground for her uncoordinated legs
And top-heavy torso.
Trying to swim through invisible water,
Our self-amusing baby
Moves backward, like a crawfish,
Then ahead, like a sea horse.
Noise doesn't disrupt her concentration.
After sleep, at play, before feeding,
She pantomimes center-stage antics,
With the ceremonial theatrics
Of a vaudevillian.

Her prairie-reared grandparents
Remain entranced,
Her performance evoking reveries
Of their own childhoods.
As they watch her, their days unravel
Like threads in the bedspread
Beneath the girl
Whose eyes beguile them
Into the delicate dream her mind weaves
Almost as though she knows
They've also upstaged similar audiences,
With the unsyncopated timing
Heritage bestows on child actors
Starring in mankind's oldest traveling show.

The Dream Tree

I

Beyond Earth,
On the planet of Zilla,
There lived a baby, Silly Nardilla,

Who envisioned a tree
Draped with namels and nakes,
Nippos, crackoons, grators, and nowls,

Not old St. Nick's
Traditional Christmas trimmings.
She prayed, all year long,

That her wishes would be heard
In the far-distant gardens,
Where peaceable-kingdom creatures

Slumber serenely, side by side,
In a very green forest.
Leones, ostricks, *tigres*, and tortoyses,

Even her sagacious friends,
Those slow-moving pachyderms
Undulant and Silliphant,

Heard pleas she made,
Kneeling at her bedside, each evening,
Before elves lullabied her to sleep.

II

Deep in Trilogy Maya's mind,
A meeting was convened.
When all the animals reached agreement

About the roles they'd play
On Christmas Eve,
They boarded Noah's Ark

And floated her gardenia-streams
Of dreamy dreams.
Finally, they arrived safely at the hour

When she awakened, in surprise,
To find all those gifts she'd desired,
Arrayed on the floor, around her.

And in the tree's branches,
The animals who'd come to visit her
Became lights kissing her eyes,

Future friends come alive,
To share in her excited delight,
On this, her first earthly celebration

Of eternal love. Entranced,
Her parents stood silently nigh,
As their baby unwrapped her fantasies.

Just Crawling

Our baby moves like an ameba.
She crawls, sits, falls over,
Then takes up a new direction,
Achieving a distance, measured in feet,
Across a Persian rug,
Before tumbling like a bear cub,

As she reaches, strains, totters sideways,
In a skydiver's slow roll,
While negotiating between smiles
And wide-eyed sighs
Of relief and disbelief.
Trilogy is the sum of her energy,

What we, her parents, recognize
As an extension of our own mentalities.
Her being calls all eyes
To crawl with her, on bended knees,
Up trees whose leaves are snowflakes
Or spider webs of gold and green.

Little Soul

You're a little soul growing older,
Trilogy Maya,
Grabbing toes peeking from sandals,
Plastic beads,
Anything that just might fit
Between your teething gums.
Now, you're sitting up
Without leaning,
Crawling without resting
Every few feet,
Reaching for walls and tables,
To steady your flabby legs,
Not quite ready
To walk on your own.
You're a little soul growing older,
Trilogy Maya,
Coalescing as your glowing spirit
Overflows with love.

Growing Familiar

Not Only a Matter of Love

I awaken to a house full of baby
Gabbling on Sunday morning's first floor.
Her bibble-de-babble reminds me
Of a cantor chanting, in Hebrew,
Or a rooster cock-a-doodle-doing to the dawn.

The sounds are the growing child
Absorbed in daytime play,
Who's briefly engaged, as a researcher,
In the pursuit of elusive answers.
Her fascinations are transitory fixations

In a dream machine she's perfecting
As her eyes, fingers, and supple brain
Formulate each new encounter
In a world of Brobdingnagian objects.
Within this expanding universe of hers,

We're both, at best,
The most and least common denominators.
My water seeks her level;
Hers combines with mine, unpredictably,
In rushing currents of gushing vocalizations.

We float rapids, on tongues buoyed by prattle,
Moved, exuberantly,
By the exhilarating thrill of babblement,
And end our trips, into unmapped lands,
Without translator or guide.

A precise Boswell, I keep a log,
Titled *A Gleam in the Eye*,
During her unpatterned journey toward words,
And I do so faithfully, hopefully,
As though it were only a matter of love.

The Mutoscope

A penny for my thoughts
Sets the arcade machine's reel spinning.
Its revolving picture-cards
Reveal a naked baby
Crawling in quarter time,
Stopping, frequently, to suck her thumb.

The little girl moves
As if each frame flipped
Were a rug slipped from under her,
In a shifting room;
She's infinitesimally arrested
Between cascading planes.

Suddenly, hands and knees
Have been superseded by tender feet
Arching, on tiptoes,
For her to see valleys
Beneath the furniture she fails to scale,
Fist over fist, on wobbly legs.

Such ascents
Leave her peering in every direction.
An invisible entity distracts her,
Causes her to scream a litany
Of erratic ecstasy,
Brings her, gracelessly, to her knees again.

Patiently, her mother waits,
Somewhere beyond the final frames,
For cues that Trilogy is tiring
And ready to be put to bed,
Where she'll escape from the circular path
That rims her days.

I desperately fumble for a penny,
To keep the reel spinning,
But by the time I find one,
The cards have reached their end,
And the hot light has faded.
Trilogy is fast alseep.

Soccer Practice

The notion of Trilogy crawling on all fours
Recalls the stupendous energy I expended
During my days in training for soccer,
Frustrations of failing to score
Right in front of the goal,
Falling to frozen ground,
From a blind-side collision,
Grasping at space, or dodging a tackle,
To avoid being kicked in the shins,
Getting my vulnerable bones bruised
Unmercifully.

Suddenly, the match is being replayed,
On our living-room floor,
With referees on the sidelines.
She dashes past,
All by herself, in open field,
Balancing her noisy blur,
Racing toward the posts — chair legs.
Awkwardly, she zeroes in, kicks,
Becomes the victory ball I catch,
Behind the goal line,
In the net of my outstretched arms.

Entering Ten Months

She's a chipmunk with puffy cheeks,
Who exposes three upper teeth, two below,
When she decides to smile —
All five rare opals,
Shining perpetually.

She opens and closes drawers and doors,
Challenges mountainous sofas,
Escapes imaginary enemies,
Through passes she locates
Behind tables and chairs.

Every floor is a field for unrehearsed sport,
Where she's constantly absorbed in games
With exotically shaped objects
From the Kingdom of Things:
Winged whirligigs and brass rings.

Often, she'll demolish a basketful
Of freshly washed and folded clothes,
Throwing each piece over her shoulder,
Only to find, surprisedly,
A pile rising behind her.

We laugh at ourselves,
For having created such outrageous companionship,
Then cavort with her, playing peekaboo,
Hiding our eyes behind nothing
But the lighted corners of her mind.

Whenever she peers out,
To see if we're still there,
We're exactly where she left us, smiling.
Finally, sleep-spells beguile her,
And she senses herself

Being drawn gently away from play.
Softly, she trills a coda
Familiar to her mother's ears,
Before a sweet stillness
Overtakes all her furious activity.

During her brief naps,
We wait outside her door of dreams,
For each new awakening.
Oh, what a precious renascence
The three of us anticipate after every hiatus.

Gentle Lamentations

Preposterously yellow forsythias
Sear the eyes, to ecstasy.
Like slowly inflating balloons,
Trees, everywhere,
Fill out with gauzy green hues, blooming,

And I'm reminded of my wife,
A year ago,
Nearing the end of pregnancy,
Flush with her lush blossom
Rushing, headlong, from May's bud.

Last April, we shared, with spring,
The secret of beginnings,
Choosing, unanimously, harmoniously,
The name "Trilogy Maya,"
For the fruit of our sweetest harvest.

Now, the outrageous forsythias frustrate us,
With their flaunting ways,
Taunt us to renew the covenant
We made with nature, last May,
One we can't possibly repeat, this season.

The Golden Chain

Sweet Trilogy is on her way,
Wearing rompers
Or gay-colored pinafores,
Everywhere bustling.
She's a genie,
Fancifully freed on the heartland,
Entertaining us with her quick changes.

Her first birthday imminent,
Her second spring sprung,
She's become a piece of the seasons,
Recapitulating
And reshaping echoes
Connecting our trilogy to God,
By an invisible umbilical cord,

And God to every generation
That has perpetuated itself in us,
Through compassion and love.
The greening leaves are ancestors
Returning to observe her rebirth,
As she lengthens the chain of being
By one infrangible link.

Forebears

So far from the city
Yet still so near
When grandparents grow lonesome,
She has merely to dream herself there,
And the sullied city air will part,
Like waters of the Red Sea,
To let her pass from the country, unscathed.

We're her immediate link to them,
And they her guarantee
That those who procreated us
Will yet be perpetuated
Through memories of our family's heritage,
Long after she's met and married
The husband of her years.

Biographical Note

Louis Daniel Brodsky was born in St. Louis, Missouri, in 1941, where he attended St. Louis Country Day School. After earning a B.A., magna cum laude, at Yale University in 1963, he received an M.A. in English from Washington University in 1967 and an M.A. in Creative Writing from San Francisco State University the following year.

From 1968 to 1987, while continuing to write poetry, he assisted in managing a 350-person men's-clothing factory in Farmington, Missouri, and started one of the Midwest's first factory-outlet apparel chains. From 1980 to 1991, he taught English and creative writing, part-time, at Mineral Area College, in nearby Flat River. Since 1987, he has lived in St. Louis and devoted himself to composing poems and short fictions. He has a daughter and a son.

Brodsky is the author of sixty-two volumes of poetry (five of which have been published in French by Éditions Gallimard) and twenty-three volumes of prose, including nine books of scholarship on William Faulkner and seven books of short fictions. His poems and essays have appeared in *Harper's*, *Faulkner Journal*, *Southern Review*, *Texas Quarterly*, *National Forum*, *American Scholar*, *Studies in Bibliography*, *Kansas Quarterly*, *Forum*, *Cimarron Review*, and *Literary Review*, as well as in *Ariel*, *Acumen*, *Orbis*, *New Welsh Review*, *Dalhousie Review*, and other journals. His work has also been printed in five editions of the *Anthology of Magazine Verse and Yearbook of American Poetry*.

In 2004, Brodsky's *You Can't Go Back, Exactly* won the award for best book of poetry, presented by the Center for Great Lakes Culture, at Michigan State University.

Other Poetry and Short Fictions Available from Time Being Books

Yakov Azriel
Beads for the Messiah's Bride: Poems on Leviticus
In the Shadow of a Burning Bush: Poems on Exodus
Threads from a Coat of Many Colors: Poems on Genesis

Edward Boccia
No Matter How Good the Light Is: Poems by a Painter

Louis Daniel Brodsky
The Capital Café: Poems of Redneck, U.S.A.
Catchin' the Drift o' the Draft *(short fictions)*
Combing Florida's Shores: Poems of Two Lifetimes
The Complete Poems of Louis Daniel Brodsky: Volumes One–Four
Dine-Rite: Breakfast Poems
Disappearing in Mississippi Latitudes: Volume Two of *A Mississippi Trilogy*
The Eleventh Lost Tribe: Poems of the Holocaust
Falling from Heaven: Holocaust Poems of a Jew and a Gentile *(Brodsky and Heyen)*
Forever, for Now: Poems for a Later Love
Four and Twenty Blackbirds Soaring
Gestapo Crows: Holocaust Poems
Leaky Tubs *(short fictions)*
Mississippi Vistas: Volume One of *A Mississippi Trilogy*
Mistress Mississippi: Volume Three of *A Mississippi Trilogy*
Nuts to You! *(short fictions)*
Once upon a Small-Town Time: Poems of America's Heartland
Paper-Whites for Lady Jane: Poems of a Midlife Love Affair
Peddler on the Road: Days in the Life of Willy Sypher
Pigskinizations *(short fictions)*
Rated Xmas *(short fictions)*
Shadow War: A Poetic Chronicle of September 11 and Beyond, Volumes One–Five
Showdown with a Cactus: Poems Chronicling the Prickly Struggle
   Between the Forces of Dubya-ness and Enlightenment, 2003–2006
Still Wandering in the Wilderness: Poems of the Jewish Diaspora
This Here's a Merica *(short fictions)*
The Thorough Earth
Three Early Books of Poems by Louis Daniel Brodsky, 1967–1969: *The Easy
   Philosopher, "A Hard Coming of It" and Other Poems*, and *The Foul Rag-
   and-Bone Shop*
Toward the Torah, Soaring: Poems of the Renascence of Faith
A Transcendental Almanac: Poems of Nature
Voice Within the Void: Poems of *Homo supinus*
The World Waiting to Be: Poems About the Creative Process

866-810-1884
http://www.timebeing.com

Louis Daniel Brodsky *(continued)*
Yellow Bricks *(short fictions)*
You Can't Go Back, Exactly

Harry James Cargas *(editor)*
Telling the Tale: A Tribute to Elie Wiesel on the Occasion of His 65th
  Birthday — Essays, Reflections, and Poems

Judith Chalmer
Out of History's Junk Jar: Poems of a Mixed Inheritance

Gerald Early
How the War in the Streets Is Won: Poems on the Quest of Love and Faith

Gary Fincke
Blood Ties: Working-Class Poems

Charles Adés Fishman
Blood to Remember: American Poets on the Holocaust *(editor)*
Chopin's Piano

CB Follett
Hold and Release

Albert Goldbarth
A Lineage of Ragpickers, Songpluckers, Elegiasts & Jewelers: Selected
  Poems of Jewish Family Life, 1973–1995

Robert Hamblin
From the Ground Up: Poems of One Southerner's Passage to Adulthood
Keeping Score: Sports Poems for Every Season

William Heyen
Erika: Poems of the Holocaust
Falling from Heaven: Holocaust Poems of a Jew and a Gentile *(Brodsky and Heyen)*
The Host: Selected Poems, 1965–1990
Pterodactyl Rose: Poems of Ecology
Ribbons: The Gulf War — A Poem

866-842-4334
http://www.tinebeing.com

Ted Hirschfield
German Requiem: Poems of the War and the Atonement of a Third Reich Child

Virginia V. James Hlavsa
Waking October Leaves: Reanimations by a Small-Town Girl

Rodger Kamenetz
The Missing Jew: New and Selected Poems
Stuck: Poems Midlife

Norbert Krapf
Blue-Eyed Grass: Poems of Germany
Looking for God's Country
Somewhere in Southern Indiana: Poems of Midwestern Origins

Adrian C. Louis
Blood Thirsty Savages

Leo Luke Marcello
Nothing Grows in One Place Forever: Poems of a Sicilian American

Gardner McFall
The Pilot's Daughter
Russian Tortoise

Joseph Meredith
Hunter's Moon: Poems from Boyhood to Manhood

Ben Milder
The Good Book Also Says . . . : Numerous Humorous Poems Inspired by
   the New Testament
The Good Book Says . . . : Light Verse to Illuminate the Old Testament
Love Is Funny, Love Is Sad
What's So Funny About the Golden Years
The Zoo You Never Gnu: A Mad Menagerie of Bizarre Beasts and Birds

Charles Muñoz
Fragments of a Myth: Modern Poems on Ancient Themes

866-810-1884
http://www.tinebeing.com

Micheal O'Siadhail
The Gossamer Wall: Poems in Witness to the Holocaust

Joseph Stanton
A Field Guide to the Wildlife of Suburban Oʻahu
Imaginary Museum: Poems on Art

Susan Terris
Contrariwise